THE
GOOD
SAMARITAN

Written by Dandi

There once lived a man
Who – a long time ago –
Set out on a trip
To the town Jericho.

When robbers jumped out
And they took all his clothes.
They beat him and left him
Confused, I suppose.

He lay by the side
Of the road that's not paved.
When a Priest passed his way,
The man thought, 'I am saved!'

Well, the man raised his head.
"Help me, Sir!" the man cried.
But the Priest turned his head
And walked off to the side.

'It's all over,' he thought.
Then, how his hopes soared
When he spotted a Rabbi!
He screamed, "Praise the Lord!"

But that Rabbi was busy
With plans for the day;
So he just crossed the street
And then hurried away.

One last person chanced by,
The man strained to see.
'Just my luck! A Samaritan –
No help for me!'

'For Samaritans hate me,
And I hate them too.
He will kill me himself
Like Samaritans do!'

But to his great surprise
That Samaritan stayed.
Then he bandaged his wounds
And said, "Don't be afraid."

Next, he lifted the man
To his very own beast,
And he led him to safety
And ordered a feast.

The Samaritan bid
The Innkeeper, "Take care.
For this man is my brother.
I'll pay what is fair."

Yes, we all are just neighbors.
Let's all be a friend.
It was Jesus who taught us
This story. The End.

 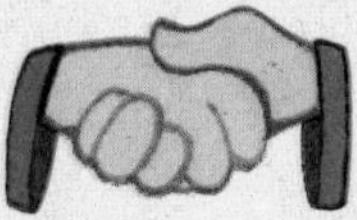 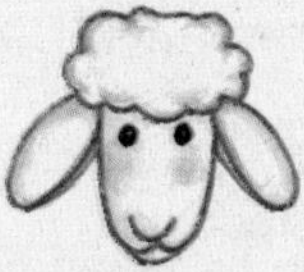